G000280496

A Woman of
No Importance

A monologue from *Talking Heads*

Alan Bennett

Samuel French—London
New York-Toronto-Hollywood

A WOMAN OF NO IMPORTANCE

First shown on BBC TV on 19th November 1982. The cast was as follows:

Peggy   Patricia Routledge

Directed by Giles Foster
Produced by Innes Lloyd
Designed by Vic Meredith

Subsequently performed as part of the stage version of *Talking Heads*, which opened on 28th January 1992. The cast was as follows:

Peggy   Patricia Routledge

Directed by Alan Bennett
Designed by Simon Higlett

AUTHOR'S NOTES

Scenery

No attempt should be made to make the setting realistic. There should be no unnecessary decoration, and no furniture additional to that needed in the action.

Lighting

In order to avoid applause, the lights should fade between each section of the play, as indicated, but not to black-out, the only black-out being at the end of the play. The performer should be visible in the fade as sometimes there is relevant action between the scenes.

Other plays by Alan Bennett published by
Samuel French Ltd:

Enjoy

Getting On

Habeas Corpus

Kafka's Dick (revised)

Office Suite:
Green Forms *and* A Visit from Miss Prothero

The Old Country

Single Spies:
An Englishman Abroad *and* A Question
of Attribution

Talking Heads:
A Chip in the Sugar *and* A Lady of Letters

A WOMAN OF NO IMPORTANCE

At the back of the stage is a flat, plain but with, perhaps, a dado rail to suggest a hospital. A locker stands in front of the flat, to the R, with a vase of anemones and several 'Get Well' cards face down on it. There is a radiator DL. A plain upright chair — which should not look out of place in the home or in a hospital — is placed C

Peggy is a middle-aged woman. She sits on the chair, her handbag on her lap, facing the audience

Peggy I was all right on the Monday. I was all right on the Tuesday. And I was all right on the Wednesday until lunchtime, at which point all my nice little routine went out of the window.

Normally, i.e. provided Miss Hayman isn't paying us one of her state visits, come half-past twelve and I'm ready to down tools and call it a morning. I put on a lick of paint, slip over and spend a penny in Costing — I should technically use the one in Records but I've told them, that lavatory seat is a death trap. And I'm not ringing up again. 'Try a bit of sellotape.' What are they paid for? I'll then rout out Miss Brunskill from four-o-two and we'll meander gently over for our midday meal. But you just have to hit it right because, give it another five minutes, and believe me, that canteen is dog eat dog.

However, if you can manage to nip in before the avalanche you have the pick of the tables and there's still a semblance of hygiene. Our particular stamping ground is just the other side of the bamboo framework thing they tried to grow ivy up. It's what Miss Brunskill calls 'our little backwater'. We're more or less fixtures there and have been for yonks. In fact Mr Skidmore came by with his tray last week just as we were concluding our coffee and he said, 'Well, girls, fancy seeing you!' We laughed. Girls! Mr Skidmore generally gravitates to the table in the far corner under that silly productivity thermometer-type thing. 'Export or Die!' It's actually broken — stuck anyway — but it's where management tend to foregather since we've had this absurd 'All Barriers Down' policy. Once upon a time management had tables roped off. That's gone, only they still congregate there. 'Huddling together for warmth,' Mr Rudyard calls it. I said to Mr Cresswell, 'You can tell who's an activist.' We laughed, because anybody more conformist than Mr Rudyard you couldn't want, and he has beautiful fingernails. Of course once the management started frequenting that particular table sure enough Miss Hayman and the Personnel brigade pitch camp next door. And she'll turn around and chat to Mr Skidmore over the back of her chair. She never used to have all that hair.

Our table though we're very much the happy family. There's me, Miss Brunskill, Mr Cresswell and Mr Rudyard, Pauline Lucas, who's ex-Projects ... to tell the truth she's still Projects, only she's in Presentation wearing her Projects hat. Then there's Trish Trotter (when she's not in one of her 'bit of cheese and an apple' phases); Joy Pedley pays us the occasional visit, but by and large that's the hard core. Trish Trotter is the only one with a right weight problem but we're all salad fanatics and keep one another in line. I have to watch my stomach anyway and salad suits Miss Brunskill because she's a big Christian Scientist. But to add that bit of excitement I bring along some of my home-made French dressing. Mr Cresswell keeps pestering me to give Mr Rudyard what he calls 'the secret formula'. He's a keen cook, Mr Rudyard. Little moustache, back like a ramrod, you'd never guess it. I pretend there's a mystery ingredient and won't let on. We laugh.

People are a bit envious of us, I know. I ran into Mr McCorquodale the other day when we were both queueing in (guess!) Accounts and he said 'You do seem to have a good time on your table, Peggy. What do you talk about?' And I didn't know. I mean, what do we talk about? Pauline's mother keeps getting a nasty rash that affects her elbows and we'd been discussing that. Mr Cresswell and Mr Rudyard were going in for some new curtains for their lounge and were debating about whether to have Thames Green. And I was saying if Thames Green was the green I thought it was I liked it in a front door but wasn't keen on it in curtains. So that made for some quite lively discussion. And Trish Trotter had got hold of some new gen on runner beans as part of a calorie-controlled diet, and we kicked that around for a bit. But honestly, that was all it was. I don't know what we do talk about half the time! My secret is, I don't talk about myself. When Joy Pedley went to Thirsk on a 'Know Your Client' course that was apparently the whole gist of it: concentrate on the other person. I said,'Well, I've no need to go to Thirsk to learn that. It's something I've been born with.' We laughed.

Once we've lined up our eats and got the table organized Miss B. gets her nose into her crossword while I scan the horizon for the rest of the gang. I have to be on my toes because there's always some bright spark wanting to commandeer them and drag them off elsewhere. I don't think people like to see other people enjoying themselves, basically. Take Pauline Lucas. The other day, she came in with young Stuart Selby. He's ginger, and when Mr Oyston went up into Accounts and Mrs Ramaroop moved to Keighley, Stuart did a bit of a dog's hind leg and got into Costing. Him and Pauline were making a bee-line for the window, which is in the Smoking area. Now Pauline doesn't smoke, in fact rather the reverse. So I sang out 'You're not deserting us, are you, Pauline? Fetch Stuart over here. See how the other half lives!' So she did. Only halfway he ran into Wendy Walsh and it ended up just being me and Pauline. I said to her, 'That was a narrow escape.' She said,'Yes'. We laughed. Her acne's heaps better.

And then look at Mr Cresswell and Mr Rudyard. It's the biggest wonder last week they didn't get sat with the truck drivers. They were dawdling past with their trays and there was room but luckily I just happened to be going past *en route* for some coffee and saw which way the wind was blowing and rescued them in the nick of time. I said, "You two! You don't know you're born!' They laughed.

However, as I say, on this particular Wednesday I'm in the office, it's half-past twelve and I'm just thinking, 'Time you were getting your skates on, Peggy,' when suddenly the door opens and nobody comes in. I didn't even look up. I just said, 'Yes, Mr Slattery?' He was on his hands and knees with a pro forma in his mouth. Anybody else would have got up. Not him. He crawls up to me, pretending to be a dog and starts begging, this bit of paper in his mouth! I thought,'You're a grown man. You've got a son at catering college; your wife's in and out of mental hospital and you're begging like a dog.' I enjoy a joke, but I didn't laugh.

Surprise, surprise he's after a favour. The bit of paper is the Squash Ladder. Would I run him off two dozen copies? I said, 'Yes. By all means. At two o'clock.' He said, 'No. Now.' Wants to put them round in the lunch hour. I said, 'Sorry, no can do.' I haven't forgotten the works outing. Running around with that thing on his head. He was like a crazed animal. I said, 'Anybody with an atom of consideration would have come down earlier. Squash Ladder! It's half-past twelve.' He said, 'It's not for me.' I said, 'Who's it for?' He said, 'Mr Skidmore.'

Pause

Well, as luck would have it I hadn't actually switched the machine off. And, knowing Trevor Slattery, Mr Skidmore had probably asked him to do it first thing and he'd only just got round to it. I know Mr Skidmore, courtesy is his middle name. But it did mean I didn't get out of the office until twenty to, by which time of course there's no Miss Brunskill. Any delay and La Brunskill's off like a shot from a gun, plastic hip or no plastic hip.

By this time of course the canteen is chock-a-block. I was five minutes just getting inside the door, and if I'd waited for a please or thank you I'd be stood there yet. They looked to be about to introduce martial law around the salad bowl so I thought, 'Little adventure, I'll opt for the hot dish of the day, steak bits or chicken pieces.' I knew the woman doling it out because she gets on the fifty-six. She's black but I take people as they come, and seeing it was me she scrapes me up the last of the steak bits. I topped it off with some mushrooms, and trust me if I didn't get the last of the yogurts as well. I heard someone behind me say, 'Damn.' I laughed.

I beetled over to our table but no Pauline, no Mr Cresswell and no Mr Rudyard. It's a cast of unknowns and only Miss Brunskill that I recognize. I said, 'Didn't you save me a place?' She said, 'I thought you'd been and gone.' Been and gone? How could I have been and gone, she knows I'm meticulous. But I just said, 'Oh' rather pointedly, and started touring round.

Eventually I pinpoint Pauline sat with little Stuart Selby, only there's no room there either. 'Scattered to the four winds today, Pauline,' I said. 'Yes,' she said, and he laughed. I see she's starting another spot.

I trek over to the far side and blow me if Mr Cresswell and Mr Rudyard aren't sat there with all the maintenance men, some of them still in their overalls. Mr Cresswell is smoking between courses, something he never does with us, a treacle sponge just stuck there, waiting. Mr Rudyard is having a salad and I wave my jar of French dressing in case he wants some but he doesn't see me because for some reason he's not wearing his glasses.

Just then I spot somebody vacating a place up at the top end. I say, 'Room for a little one?', only nobody takes on. They're young, mostly from Design, moustaches and those little T-shirty things, having some silly conversation about a topless Tandoori restaurant. I start on my steak bits, only to find that what she's given me is mainly gristle. I don't suppose they distinguish in Jamaica. I thought, 'Well, I'll have a little salt, perk it up a bit', but as luck would have it there's none on the table, so I get up again and go in quest of some. The first salt I spot is on the table opposite, which happens to be the table patronized by the management; and who should be sat there but Mr Skidmore. So I asked him if I could borrow their salt. 'Excuse me, Mr Skidmore,' was what I said, 'but could I relieve you temporarily of your salt?' I saw Miss Hayman's head come round. She'd naturally think I was crawling. I wasn't. I just wanted some salt. Anyway, Mr Skidmore was very obliging. 'By all means,' he said. 'Would you like the pepper too?' I said, 'That's most civil of you, but I'm not a great pepper fan.' So I just took the salt, put a bit on the side of my plate and took it back. 'Much obliged,' I said. 'Don't mention it,' Mr Skidmore said. 'Any time.' He has impeccable manners, they have a big detached house at Alwoodley, his wife has had a nervous breakdown, wears one of those sheepskin coats.

I suddenly bethought me of the Squash Ladder, so just after I'd replaced the salt I said, 'Oh, by the way, I ran you off those copies of the Squash Ladder,' not in a loud voice, just person to person. He said, 'What?' I said, 'I ran you off those copies of the Squash

Ladder.' He said, 'Squash Ladder?' I said 'Yes.' He said, 'Not my pigeon.' I said, 'Why?' He said, 'Don't you know? There's been a flare-up with my hernia.' Well I didn't know. I can't see how I would be expected to know. Somebody laughed. I said, 'Oh, I am sorry.' He said, 'I'm not. Blessing in disguise. Squash is Slattery's pigeon now.'

I went back to my table and sat down. I felt really sickened. He'd done it on me had Mr Slattery.

After a bit Trish Trotter rolls up and parks herself next to me. She says, 'Are you not eating your steak bits?' I said, 'No.' She said, 'Don't mind if I do,' and helps herself. She shouldn't wear trousers.

Anyway it was that afternoon that I first began to feel really off it. I went home at half-past four.

Music plays and the Lights fade, but not to Black-out; Peggy is still visible as:

   She rises and exits to the right of the flat. She returns, without her jacket and carrying a mug of tea, and sits again

The music fades; the Lights return to normal

I don't run to the doctor every five minutes. On the last occasion Dr Copeland sat me down and said, 'Miss Schofield. If I saw my other patients as seldom as I see you I should be out of business.' We laughed.

He's always pleased to see me: gets up when I come into the room, sits me down, then we converse about general topics for a minute or two before getting down to the nub of the matter. He has a picture of his children on his desk, taken years ago because the son's gone to Canada now and his daughter's an expert in man-made fibres. He never mentions his wife, I think she left him, he has a sensitive face. Cactuses seem to be his sideline. There's always one on his desk and he has a Cactus Calendar hung up. This month's was somewhere in Arizona, huge, a man stood beside it, tiny. I looked at it while he was diddling his hands after the previous patient.

There was a young man in the room and Dr Copeland introduced me. He said, 'This is Miss ...' (he was looking at my notes) '... Miss Schofield. Mr Metcalf is a medical student; he's mistaken enough to want to become a doctor.' We laughed, but the boy kept a straight face. He had on one of those zip-up cardigans I think a bit common so that didn't inspire confidence. Dr Copeland said would I object to Mr Metcalf conducting the examination provided he was standing by to see I came to no actual physical harm? We both laughed but Mr Metcalf was scratching a mark he'd found on the knee of his trousers.

Dr Copeland put him in the picture about me first: 'Miss Schofield has been coming to me over a period of twelve years. Her health is generally good, wouldn't you say Miss Schofield?—' and he was going on, but I interjected. I said, 'Well, it is good,' I said, 'but it's quite likely to seem better than it is because I don't come running down to the surgery with every slightest thing.' 'Yes,' he said. 'If I saw my other patients as seldom as I see Miss Schofield I should be out of business.' He laughed. The student then asked me what the trouble was and I went through the saga of the steak bits and my subsequent tummy upset.

He said, 'Is there anything besides that?' I said, 'No.' He said, 'Any problems at work?' I said, 'No.' He said, 'Any problems at home?' I said, 'No.' He said, 'You're single.' I said, 'Yes.' He said, 'Where are your parents?' I said, 'Mother's in her grave and father is in a Sunshine Home at Moortown.' He said, 'Do you feel bad about that?' (He didn't look more than seventeen.) I said, 'No. Not after the life he's lived.'

I saw him look at Dr Copeland, only he was toying with the calendar, sneaking a look at what next month's cactus was going to be. So this youth said, 'What life did he lead?' I said, 'A life that involved spending every other weekend at Carnforth with a blondified piece from the cosmetics counter at Timothy White's and Taylor's.' He said, 'Is that a shoe shop?' I said, 'You're thinking of Freeman, Hardy and Willis. It's a chemist. Or was. It's been taken over by Boots. And anyhow she now has a little gown shop at Bispham. His previous was a Meltonian shoe cream demonstrator at Manfield's, and what has this to do with my stomach?'

Dr Copeland said, 'Quite. I think it's about time you took an actual look at the patient, Metcalf.' So the young man examined me, the way they do, pressing his hands into me and whatnot, and then calls over Dr Copeland to have a look. 'That's right,' I said. 'Make way for the expert.' Only neither of them laughed.

Dr Copeland kneaded me about a bit, but more professionally and while he was washing his hands he said, 'Miss Schofield. I'm not in the least bit worried by your stomach. But, you being you, it wants looking at. There aren't many of us left!' We laughed. 'So just to be on the safe side I want to make an appointment for you to see a specialist, Mr Penry-Jones.' I said, 'Isn't his wife to do with the music festival?' He said, 'I don't know, is she?' I said, 'She is. I've seen a picture of her talking to Lord Harewood.'

She rises and moves R, *slightly upstage*

He took me to the door of the consulting room, which he doesn't do with everybody, and he took my hand. (I'm not a private patient.) 'Thank you,' he said. 'Thank you for being a guinea pig.' We laughed. Only it's funny, just as I was coming out I saw the student's face and he was looking really pleased with himself.

She very slightly presses her hand into her stomach

Music plays and the Lights fade, but not completely

Peggy exits UR and returns from L wearing a candlewick dressing-gown and carrying a handbag and mirror. She looks at her hair in the mirror

The music fades and the Lights come up to normal

I've just had a shampoo and set. She's not done it too badly, bearing in mind she doesn't know my hair. Lois, her name is. She has a little salon. You go past Gyney, and it's smack opposite Maternity. It's a bit rudimentary, they just have it to perk up the morale of the pregnant mums basically, but, as Lois says, it's an open door policy just so long as you can find your way because the place is a rabbit warren. Lois said my hair was among the best she'd come across. It's the sort Italians make into wigs apparently, they have people scouring Europe for hair of this type.

During the following, she moves to the chair and sits

I should have had a perm last Tuesday, only when Mr Penry-Jones whipped me in here it just went by the board.

Caused chaos at work. Miss Brunskill said after I'd rung up Mr McCorquodale and Mr Skidmore went into a huddle for fully half an hour and at the end of it they still couldn't figure out a way to work round me. In the finish Miss Hayman had to come down from the fifth floor — though not wearing her Personnel hat, thank God — and Pauline did her usual sideways jump from Records, but it's all a bit pass the parcel. Miss Brunskill says everybody is on their knees praying I come back soon.

I'd actually been feeling a lot better when I went along to see Mr Penry-Jones. He's got one of those big double-fronted houses in Park Square: vast rooms, wicked to heat. There was just one woman in the waiting room, smartish, looked to have arthritis. I said, 'I wouldn't like this electricity bill,' but she just smiled. Then the housekeeper came and conducted me upstairs. I made some remark about it being spring but she didn't comment, a lot of them are Spanish these days. Mr Penry-Jones though was very courtly; oldish man, blue pin-striped suit, spotted bow tie. I said, 'What a lovely fireplace." He said, 'Yes. These are old houses.' I said, 'Georgian, I imagine.' 'Oh,' he said. 'I can see I'm in the presence of a connoisseur.' We laughed.

He examined me and I went through the story again, though I didn't actually mention the steak bits, and it was a beautiful carpet. Then he looked out of the window and asked me one or two questions about my bowels. I said, 'I believe your wife has a lot to do with the Music Festival.' He said, 'Yes.' I said, 'That must be very satisfying.' He says, 'Yes. It is. Last week she shook hands with the Queen.' I said, ' Well that's funny, because I stood as near to her as I am to you, at York in 1956. What an immaculate complexion!'

When I'd got dressed he said, 'Miss Schofield, you are a puzzle. I'm very intrigued.' I said, 'Oh?' He said, 'Have you got anything special on in the next couple of weeks?' he said. 'Because ideally what I would like to do is take you in, run a few tests and then go on from there. I'm absolutely certain there's nothing to get worked up about but we ought to have a little look. Is that all right?' I said, 'You're the doctor.' We laughed.

He made a point of coming downstairs with me. It was just as some other doctor was helping the better-class-looking woman with arthritis into a car — it looked to be chauffeur driven. I went and sat on a seat in the square for a bit before I got the bus. The trees did look nice.

Music plays; as before, the Lights fade

Peggy rises and exits R, returning from the L without her handbag but carrying a newspaper. She is still in her dressing-gown and now wears a hospital wristband with a name tag attached. She moves downstage to the L of the chair

The music fades and the Lights return to normal

I've appointed myself newspaper lady. I go round first thing taking the orders for the papers, then I nip down and intercept the trolley on its way over. I said to Sister Tudor, 'Well, with a candlewick dressing-gown I might as well.' Most of the others have these silly shorty things. Mine's more of a housecoat. The shade was called Careless Pink, only that's fifteen years ago. It's mostly the *Sun* or the *Mirror*, there's only two of us get the *Mail* and she's another Miss.

During the following she moves the chair R of the cabinet and stands R of the chair

I could tell straight away she was a bit more refined. Hysterectomy.

Of course I shan't be able to do the papers tomorrow because of my op.

When Princess Alexandra came round, this was the bed she stopped at, apparently.

I get on like a house on fire with the nurses. We do laugh. Nurse Trickett says I'm their star patient. She's little and a bit funny-looking but so good-hearted. 'How's our star patient?' she says. 'I hope you've been behaving yourself.' We laugh. She hasn't got a boyfriend. I've promised to teach her shorthand typing. Her mother has gallstones, apparently. Nurse Gillis is the pretty one. I think she's just marking time until she finds the right man. And then there's Nurse Conkie, always smiling. I said to her, 'You're always smiling, you're a lesson to any shop steward, you.' She laughed and laughed the way they do when they're black.

Sister came in while she was laughing and said wasn't it time Mrs Boothman was turned over. She's all right is Sister, but she's like me: she has a lot on her plate. I said to her, 'I'm a professional woman myself.' She smiled.

Pause. Peggy turns the name tag she has on her wrist

Name on my wrist now: 'Schofield, Margaret, Miss.'

Pause

Mr Penry-Jones comes round on a morning, and he fetches his students and they have to guess what's wrong. I said to Miss Brunskill, 'It's a bit of a game. If he doesn't't know what the matter is, they won't.' He said, 'Gentlemen, a big question mark hangs over Miss Schofield's stomach.' They all laughed.

So, tomorrow's the big day. He was telling the students what he's going to do. 'I'm just going to go in,' he said, ' and have a look round.

We're not going to do anything, just a tour of inspection.' I chipped in, 'More of a guided tour, if these are there.' They did *laugh*. Not Sister, though. She can't afford to, I suppose. He's like a god to them, Mr Penry-Jones.

I do my bit here in different ways. I'm always going round the beds, having a word, particularly when someone isn't mobile. I run them little errands and tell the nurse if there's anything anybody's wanting. Mrs Maudsley opposite's on a drip and she was going on about getting her toenails cut, they catch on the sheet. I located Nurse Gillis and told her, only it must have slipped her mind because when I went across later on Mrs Maudsley was still on about it. I mentioned it again to Nurse Gillis just in case she'd forgotten and she said, 'I don't know how we managed before you came, Miss Schofield, I honestly don't.' Actually I found out later her toenails *had* been cut. Apparently Nurse Conkie must have cut them the same day as she cut mine, the day before yesterday, only Mrs Maudsley wouldn't know because she's no feeling in her feet.

Mrs Boothman's another of my regulars. Can't move. Can't speak. Doesn't bother me. I sit and chat away to her as if it was the most normal thing in the world. She'll sometimes manage a little movement of her hand, but the look in her eyes is enough.

Miss Brunskill's been down to see me. Nobody else much. Plenty of cards. I've got more cards than anybody else on this side.

She picks up the pile of cards and goes through them, setting each one up on the locker as she talks about it

'Feel kinda sick without you. Trish.' Trish Trotter. Picture of an elephant. 'Wishing you a speedy recovery. All in four-o-six.' 'It's not the same without you. You're missed more than words can tell. so I'm sending this card to say, Please hurry and get well.' It says

'From all on the fifth floor,' but I bet it's Mr Skidmore, it's such a classy card. A thatched cottage. I should imagine it can be damp, though, thatch. Silly one from Mr Cresswell and Mr Rudyard. 'Sorry you're sick. Hope you'll soon be back to normal. Whatever that is!'

I thought they might have been popping down, but Mr Cresswell hates hospitals, apparently, and they're going in for a new dog. A Dandy Dinmont. They think it'll be company for Tina, their Jack Russell. Well, they're out all day.

Pause

Miss Brunskill's knitting me a bedjacket. I said, 'You'll have to be sharp, I shall be home next week.'

Pause

Could just drink a cup of tea. Can't when you're having an op. They get you up at six, apparently. Give you a jab. Nurse Trickett says I won't even know I've gone and I'll be back up here by twelve. I've warned Sister I shan't be able to get the papers, she thinks they'll manage.

Pause

Solve the mystery anyway.

Music plays and the Lights fade

> *Peggy gets up and exits* R, *returning from* L *in a wheelchair with a blanket over her knees. She wheels herself downstage and stops by the radiator* DL

The music fades; the Lights return to normal

Hair in my dinner again today. Second time this week. Someone must be moulting. I mentioned it to Sister and she said she'd take it up with the kitchen staff and get back to me. She hasn't, though. It isn't that she's nasty. Just crisp. I don't complain. Nurse Gillis can be sharp as well, but I try and meet her half way. I said, 'Don't apologize. I deal with people myself. They don't realize, do they?'

Pause

I'd such a shock yesterday. Nurse Conkie and Nurse Trickett had just given me my bath, and the little trainee nurse with the bonny face and cold hands was combing my hair, when I bethought me of the little bedjacket Miss Brunskill had knitted me. I'd put it away in my locker because she'd made it too tight round the sleeves, but I tried it on again and it was just right. She says she hates knitting. I'm the only person she'll knit for, apparently. Of course, I paid for the wool. She's never ailed a thing, Miss Brunskill. Still, I hadn't until this do. Anyway I'd just got the bedjacket on and she'd fetched Nurse Conkie to see how nice I looked and they got me out my lipstick and I put a bit of that on. I was just sitting there and Nurse Conkie said, ' All dressed up and nowhere to go,' and a voice said, 'Hallo. Long time no see!' And it's Mr Skidmore!

And I said it, loud, like that, 'Mr Skidmore!' I said to him, I said, 'Five minutes earlier and you'd have seen me being bathed.' He said, 'That's the story of my life.' We laughed.

He chatted about work. Said they were still only limping along. Said my job is open whenever I feel up to it and what's more it'll stay that way. They've got a special dispensation from Mr Strudwick. He says it's open-ended. They've never done that before. When Wendy Walsh had her infected sinus they ended up giving her a deadline. Still, she wasn't the linch-pin I am.

He did say there were other factors quite unconnected pushing them towards some degree of revamping. 'But,' he said, and patted my hand, 'in that event we shall find you a niche.' I said, ' Well, I'm honoured. Fancy making a special journey for me.' Only it transpires that Mrs Skidmore's mother is in the psychiatric ward with another of her depression do's, and he'd left Mrs Skidmore sitting with her while he popped along to see me. 'Killing two birds with one stone,' he said. Then realized. 'I didn't mean that,' he said. 'Don't be silly,' I said. We laughed. He does look young when he laughs. He'd just gone when Nurse Conkie came down to turn Mrs Boothman over. Great big smile. 'Who was your gentleman friend?' she said. She's got a nice sense of humour. I said, 'That was my boss. He says they can't wait till I'm back.' 'I'm not sure we can spare you,' she said. We laughed.

I've been here the longest now, apart from Mrs Boothman and she's been resuscitated once. I potter around doing this and that.

Mr Penry-Jones is very proud of my scar. He fetches his students round to see it nearly every week. He says he's never seen a scar heal as quickly as mine. It's to do with the right mental attitude apparently. They stop longer at my bed than with anybody. What he does is take the students a bit away, talks to them quietly, then they come up, one by one and ask me questions. I whisper to them, 'He doesn't know what it is, so don't worry if you don't.' Mrs Durrant on this side, she won't have them. She goes on about 'patients' rights'. She's a schoolteacher, though you'd never guess it to look at her. Long hair, masses of it. And I've heard her swear when they've given her a jab.

Pause

I have a laugh with the porters that take me down for treatment. There's one in particular, Gerald. He's always pleased when it turns

out to be me. 'My sweetheart,' he calls me. 'It's my sweetheart.'
He's black too. I get on with everybody.

Pause

I've started coming and looking out of this window. I just find it's
far enough. There's naught much to see. There's the place where
they put the bins out and a cook comes out now and again and has
a smoke. A young lad comes there with a nurse. He kisses her then
goes away. Always the same lad. Nice. Though I don't like a lot of
kissing, generally.

Pause

I keep wondering about my dad.

Music plays and the Lights fade

> *Peggy wheels the chair to face up stage. Moments later she turns
> to face down stage: she is now slumped further down in the chair,
> the blanket covering her far more, and her hair is disarranged*

The music fades and the Lights return to normal

I'm lucky. I'm standard size. I've got stuff off the peg and people
have thought I'd had it run up specially. I've got a little fawn coat
hanging up at home that I got fifteen years ago at Richard Shops. I
ring the changes with scarves and gloves and whatnot, but it's been
a grand little coat.

Pause

I fetched up ever such a lot of phlegm this morning. Nurse Gillis was
on. She was pleased. She said I'd fetched up more phlegm than

anyone else on the ward. I said, 'Was there a prize?' She laughed. I've never had that trouble before, but that's the bugbear when you're lying in bed, congestion.

Pause

She said it's a good job all the patients aren't as little trouble as me or else half the nurses would be out of work. Funny, I didn't use to like her, but she's been a lot nicer lately. Her boyfriend's a trainee something-or-other. I forget what. She did tell me. They're planning on moving to Australia.

Pause

I've never been to Australia. She said if I wanted I could come out and visit them. I said, 'Yes.' Only I wouldn't go. I couldn't be doing with all that sun.

Pause

When Princess Alexandra came round this was the bed she stopped at, apparently.

Pause

Sister's been better lately, too. The one I can't stand is Nurse Conkie. Never stops smiling. Great big smile. When they took Mrs Boothman away just the same. Great big smile.

Pause

Vicar round today. Think it was today. Beard. Sports jacket. Student, I thought, at first.

Pause

Chatted. Bit before he got round to God. Says God singles you out for suffering. If you suffer you're someone special in the eyes of God. He said he knew this from personal experience. His wife suffers from migraine.

Pause

Do without being someone special, this lot.

Pause

There's a vicar goes round at Moortown, where my dad is. Sits.

Pause

Miss Brunskill came. Revolution at work. Four-o-five and four-o-six knocked into one. Do your own photocopying now. Do it yourself, cut out the middleman. I said, 'Where did I fit in?' and she was telling me, only I must have dropped off and when I woke up she'd gone. Niche somewhere.

Pause

I've been lucky with buses when I think back. I don't know what it is but just as I get to the bus stop up comes the bus. It must be a knack. I don't think I've ever had to wait more than two minutes for a bus, even when it's been a really spasmodic service.

Pause

I wish they wouldn't laugh.

Pause

There shouldn't be laughing.

Pause

If they just left me alone I should be all right. 'Schofield, Margaret, Miss.' I've got a fly: keeps coming down. Must like me. There's a woman comes over and talks to me sometimes. Telling some tale. I close my eyes.

Pause

Somebody was telling me about Rhyl. Still very select, apparently. No crowds.

Pause

Here's my friend. This fly.

She smiles

I said to Nurse Gillis, 'It's singled me out.' She laughed.

Music plays and the Lights fade to Black-out

Peggy exits

The Lights come up again on the now empty wheelchair

CURTAIN

FURNITURE AND PROPERTY LIST

On stage: Chair
Locker. *On it*: vase of anemones, 'Get Well' cards
Radiator

Off stage: Handbag
Newspaper
Mirror
Wristband with name tag
Wheelchair
Blanket

LIGHTING PLOT

Practical fittings required: nil.
Interior. The same scene throughout

To open: General interior lighting

Cue 1	**Peggy**: '... half-past four.' *Fade lights*	(Page 7)
Cue 2	**Peggy** sits *Bring up lights*	(Page 7)
Cue 3	**Peggy** presses her stomach *Fade lights*	(Page 10)
Cue 4	**Peggy** looks at her hair in the mirror *Bring up lights*	(Page 10)
Cue 5	**Peggy**: 'The trees did look nice.' *Fade lights*	(Page 12)
Cue 6	**Peggy** moves L of the chair *Bring up lights*	(Page 12)
Cue 7	**Peggy**: 'Solve the mystery, anyway.' *Fade lights*	(Page 15)
Cue 8	**Peggy** stops by the radiator DL *Bring up lights*	(Page 15)

Cue 9   **Peggy**: 'I keep wondering about my dad.' (Page 18)
          Fade lights

Cue 10 **Peggy** turns to face down stage   (Page 18)
          Bring up lights

Cue 11 **Peggy**: 'She laughed.'   (Page 21)
          Fade lights to black-out

Cue 12 **Peggy** exits   (Page 21)
          Bring up lights

EFFECTS PLOT

Cue 1	**Peggy**: '... half-past four.' *Music*	(Page 7)
Cue 2	**Peggy** sits *Fade music*	(Page 7)
Cue 3	**Peggy** presses her stomach *Music*	(Page 10)
Cue 4	**Peggy** looks at her hair in the mirror *Fade music*	(Page 10)
Cue 5	**Peggy**: 'The trees did look nice.' *Music*	(Page 12)
Cue 6	**Peggy** moves L of the chair *Fade music*	(Page 12)
Cue 7	**Peggy**: 'Solve the mystery, anyway.' *Music*	(Page 15)
Cue 8	**Peggy** stops by the radiator DL *Fade music*	(Page 15)
Cue 9	**Peggy**: 'I keep wondering about my dad.' *Music*	(Page 18)
Cue 10	**Peggy** turns to face down stage *Fade music*	(Page 18)